Praise for *Listening as a Martial Art*

"*Listening as a Martial Art* is a game-changing book. I highly recommend it to anyone that wants to improve their performance in all areas of life."

PROF. JOHN MACHADO, 6th degree Black Belt in Brazilian Jiu-Jitsu

"A brilliant book, Cash understands what any great fighter knows that listening to your opponent is the key strategy to winning. If listening is a martial art then Cash has mastered it."

MARTIN WHEELER, Russian Martial Art, Systema (World's #1 Combatives Expert)

"Cash is one of the most creative and successful people that I call a friend. His new book about listening is an excellent manual for one of the most important components of any successful career or venture. Listening, like the martial arts, I believe, is a contact activity with many similarities to physical exchanges."

DAVID W. PRUITT, Retired Chairman and CEO of Cap Rock Energy

"A blend of Martial Arts, Dale Carnegie and business insights from Cash Nickerson....Best tips for sales professionals that I have read. Listen to your customers, don't interrupt and respond with features and benefits as the opportunities present themselves. Don't force your opinion or feed your ego and you will sell more!"

JOHN VISBAL, President, East Bay Logistics

Listening
as a
Martial Art

Listening as a Martial Art

Master Your Listening Skills for Success

Cash Nickerson

CNM Press

For information contact www.cashnickerson.com

ISBN: 978-0-9898009-3-8

First Edition

ACKNOWLEDGEMENTS

I mention a number of people who have influenced my reflections on listening, but none was more important to me personally than one of my dear friends, Cathy Colella, who died while I was writing this book. Cathy is featured in the chapter "The Beauty of Brutal Honesty." Cathy was a Ford Model who listened so well that when she gave you advice, it appeared she had gotten inside you and felt your fears and put them in front of you. My first mentor, Forrest Krutter, also recently deceased, was an incredible listener. Forrest and I worked together at Union Pacific Railroad in the mid-1980s. Forrest ended up as General Counsel for Berkshire Hathaway and Warren Buffett. Nobody listened better than Forrest.

Of course, none of my insights about martial arts and listening would have been possible without my martial arts instructors over the years. A sincere thank-you to all of my martial arts instructors—current and past. Thank you for inspiring me to write this book by teaching me how to feel others and connect physical and verbal engagement. I look forward to many more years of training with you.

TABLE OF CONTENTS

FOREWORD

I don't know how or where you spend your empty moments, those magical and precious moments when you can let your mind drift to wherever and whatever you want, whether you do it consciously or not. But I spent from December 2014 until August 2015 in those magically empty moments, just trying to think and focus on one thing: Listening. Why listening? As I reflected on the first 56 years of my life and considered who seemed to stand out in business, academic, social and interpersonal settings, I "discovered" and then remembered they had one thing in common: They were all great listeners. I have had the good fortune to interact with so many great people from every walk of life and from many countries. Listening is a differentiator and maybe the differentiator. Great leaders have it. People think of great people as speakers, writers, and active engagers in the world. But up close, they speak less than you might think. They ask and listen.

And unfortunately, as this is such a fundamental skill to learning and understanding, you would expect that you could study it and indeed that you would be required to study it. And yet I have never been offered a course in it. It is absent from our school curricula. We simply don't teach listening in any formal school setting. We teach public speaking. We teach writing. We teach reading. We teach so many things–but listening? Why not? Why and how did listening get left behind?

After considering this insight, I decided I wanted to be a great listener. I don't think I have been a great listener. At 56 I thought it would be a nice mid-career, mid-life "correction." If I couldn't be a great listener, I wanted to be at least a much better listener. But I didn't know where to turn to advance my skills. I searched the Internet. I found plenty of articles about body language. I found articles about active listening—repeating what you heard. But I found no comprehensive guide. And I wasn't looking for scholarly research. I wanted to be better. I wanted clinical information. I wanted some basic framework for improving my listening skills.

I knew from my experience that the stakes are high. People who listen better remember more. People who listen better learn better. People who listen better sell better. People who listen better have better relationships. People who listen better negotiate better. We worship speakers, but listeners rule the world.

I began my listening journey by trying to concentrate when people spoke. I tried active listening. And then one day, when I was trying so hard to listen to someone, it felt like hard work. I stared at their lips, I repeated their words in my head, I studied their gestures and body language and I was sweating, focusing so very hard. I focused so hard, I held my breath. It hurt and was stressful. I was full of tension. But then my instincts and training took over. I took a breath. I breathed in through my nose and out through my mouth. I relaxed and felt a familiar feeling, a feeling that I have felt many times before. I felt the peace that comes from martial arts practice – I felt the moment.

With that moment, that magical moment, this book was born: *Listening as a Martial Art.* It was like a lightening bolt. Dialogue is a physical interaction, just like martial arts. Combative dialogue is like sparring and great dialogue is like Tai Chi! A speech is like a beautifully performed kata (series of moves executed by some martial arts). But dialogue involves give and take and listening is like accepting an exchange.

I worked to write weekly essays about moments I felt, and the insights came quickly as the martial arts analogies and comparisons came more and more naturally. Fighting and dialogue are both human exchanges. Martial arts helps you avoid, defend and succeed in physical conflict and attacks. Listening is simply the verbal equivalent. Arguments, debates, sales and negotiations all involve points, counterpoints and evasion, just like the physical martial arts.

As with many books I write, I am not looking to be the final word or say on a subject. I am just trying to get the dialogue started. While this is a beginning, someday I dream of classes on listening and maybe even a listening institute that combines physical martial arts training with training in listening and dialogue. Regardless of the technology we invent, as hearing is one of our five senses, listening is here to stay.

As you look back on the generations and centuries before us, ask yourself, "What if we had listened to each other better?" "Wouldn't the world likely be a better place?" "Would there be fewer wars?" "Would there be less cruelty?" We are so visual. There is a tremendous amount of research that documents our over-reliance on our sense of sight. Has the domination of the visual world served us well?

As someone said, "What got us here, won't get us there." So, more than any other book I have written, this is intended to get you started, from wherever you are. I hope you join me on your own listening journey. I have developed a set of techniques to help you that may take you from a white belt to a black belt when it comes to listening. But as with any martial arts training, it is within you and up to you how well you improve your listening skills. I recommend you work on one skill a day or week or month. It will change your life no matter what your occupation, social situation or marital status. Feel free to write me and let me know how you are doing at cash@cashnickerson.com.

Godspeed in your listening journey.

INTRODUCTION

Most everyone has a mental image of martial arts. It may come from a movie like *The Karate Kid.* If you are older, it may come from Bruce Lee films or the TV series *Kung Fu.* You may have a personal relationship with martial arts or martial artists. Or maybe you have had a child in martial arts. By and large, martial arts in the United States consists of teaching techniques and katas and progressing students through belts or ranks. Martial arts is, after all, a business. But by martial arts I don't mean just memorizing techniques and katas.

True martial artists, masters and national champions, master several areas. They are like great chess players in that they are always sensing what will come next without anticipating it. They don't assume what will come at them; they are prepared for anything. They can "feel" you so well they know what you will do next before you do. They master being in "the moment." In that moment, they feel their opponent.

I have trained with so many world champions and world-class martial artists in so many disciplines. I have a 3rd-degree black belt in Kenpo Karate from Sifu Rick Fowler and have trained privately with several 9th-degree practitioners. In the process of attaining that rank I studied Shodokan Karate in the '70s in Utica, New York, and at Carleton College in Minnesota. After a hiatus I picked up Kenpo after the

9/11 attacks. I was on a plane that horrible, fateful morning in Dallas and decided I wanted to be one of those who could thwart an attack. By 2005 I had attained black-belt status, and by 2010 had advanced a couple degrees to 3rd.

In the interim, I studied kickboxing under world kickboxing champion Evan Thompson, and Jiu Jitsu under the Machado family. I started with Carlos Machado in 2007, then trained with Rigan Machado to earn a blue belt. And for the past two years I have been training with John Machado, who recently awarded me a purple belt.

Finally, and perhaps most relevant, since 2007, I have been training in Systema, the Russian Martial Art, under Vladimir Vasiliev. I also have spent a lot of time training with Martin Wheeler, a broad-based martial artist and one of the best, if not the best, in the U.S. at Systema.

I am an instructor in Systema and own a school, Big D Systema, which teaches this discipline in Irving, Texas. Martial arts is such a great hobby for a lawyer-executive type like myself because it not only forces you to relieve physical and mental tension, but also forces you to maintain your physical fitness, which gets much harder as you age. My knowledge of martial arts is deep and wide, covering 30 years of study and training, with a hiatus in the early years of my career when I thought I was too busy. That, sadly, is when we need hobbies the most.

As I have said, all the greats I have trained with have this one thing in common. They can sense what you are doing or about to do. They "feel" you. They "sense" you. They listen to your body. I have travelled to Toronto many times for seminars offered by Vladimir Vasiliev. One of my particular favorites was "Tactics of Confrontation." Vladimir could tell what someone was going to do next just by studying their body form, face and whatever else he sensed. He could do this while the person was standing there, doing nothing. He pointed out to me, "Notice how this leg is bent and the other not. If he tries to kick you, it will be with the left leg." He was right every time.

World champion Rigan Machado, whose Jiu Jitsu record is something like 400 and 0, told me he would go into tournaments with just 3 techniques. And then he would wait until the conditions presented themselves for a particular technique, then apply it. He would "listen" for the right move and then apply his submission.

This sensitivity is the result of many matches and constant study. This sensitivity is the result of many training sessions. So, like martial arts champions, you won't become a champion listener overnight. But you can get better every day and move your rank up rapidly. And someday, you can be a black-belt listener. I wish you success.

Yours in the martial arts (and listening),
Cash Nickerson
Austin, Texas
September 1, 2015

WHITE BELT

YOUR LISTENING JOURNEY BEGINS

If someone were to ask me what belt I like the most in martial arts, it is the white belt. With the white belt comes humility and openness. Great martial arts instructors know how to find out where you are without demeaning you. Great instructors know how to start you slowly so you learn how to learn, and yet give you glimpses of the practitioner you will someday become with training and practice. These first three essays are designed to lay the groundwork for what is to come. The concept of water and being like water is fundamental to martial arts. The essay *"To Listen Well Is to Be Like Water"* introduces the relationship between martial arts and listening. *"The Only Resolution You Need for Next Year"* introduces the results of listening well in one great listening practitioner, Ross Perot. It is designed to show you that successful people recognize the importance of listening. And finally, *"The Beauty of Brutal Honesty,"* which served for me and others as a public eulogy for an incredible mentor, Cathy Colella, shows you again the power of listening, and listening in particular for certain types of negative language that can prevent disasters—business or personal. As a white belt, you'll get an introduction in these chapters to listening as a martial art, and a vision of what can be accomplished with great listening.

To Listen Well Is to Be Like Water

I have dedicated myself to improving just one skill next year: Listening. I wrote "*The Only Resolution You Need for Next Year*" on December 10, 2014. During 2015, I wrote 15 essays on listening skills and this is the first in that series. Great listening is the skill that separates the great from the good, especially in sales and negotiations. So if you seek greatness, advance your listening skills. But where should you begin? Where are the guidebooks? Where are the bestsellers?

As a lifetime practicing martial artist, I find myself constantly using lessons from various martial arts to help me in the world of work. I have practiced American Kenpo Karate, Judo, Brazilian Jiu Jitsu, Kickboxing and Systema, the Russian Martial Art, in gyms, the outdoors and dojos. And I have studied many books on the martial arts including works like *The Book of Five Rings, The Demon's Sermon on the Martial Arts,* and of course, *The Tao of Jeet Kune Do.* One of the most common themes of martial arts is the silencing of your "self." Martial arts is fundamentally defensive and often arose in a culture at a time when oppressed populations weren't allowed to have weapons. Hence, the bare fists of karate (which literally means "empty hand").

To be able to defend yourself, you have to not be stressed yourself. You need to be relaxed. You need to be empty. You need to be silent. In that way, you can feel and sense others and be prepared for anything without being "blocked" by your own thoughts and senses. In a physical confrontation, if you are tense, or anticipating, or thinking about what you will do, you are much more likely to be hit by an opponent. So martial artists meditate and learn to breathe and be open. Or, as Bruce Lee said, "Be Like Water." When you are like water, you are prepared to take whatever shape you need and become what you need to become.

Suppose you are on a sales call and meeting with a prospect. Imagine you open with, "I want to sell you this and that, and here is why it is right for you, and here is why you should do it now." How does that work? You talk. If you approach your prospect in this way, you are coming "sword drawn," as it were. People try to sell me like that every day via email, voice messages, phone calls—you name it. And if you are a buyer, what do you do when someone comes at you like that? You defend yourself. Shield up! Right? As a buyer, I am on the defensive and we are already fighting. Remember, I am the one who bought the very product or service you are challenging in many cases. You are telling me why I made a bad decision last time.

Now, suppose you come with questions. You come like water. You are prepared, but not presuming why your service or product might be needed. Suppose you are selling a service. You wouldn't be there or on the phone unless you thought your service would benefit the prospect, and if they need it they are probably already buying from someone else. So what is a good question? Not "Tell me about your company." Not "How do you like your existing service?" How about "If you could change one thing about your existing service, what would it be?" Your goal is to elicit some state of dissatisfaction from your prospect that leads to an opening for you. When you open in this manner, you are letting me, the buyer, lead. I am going to feel more receptive if it is my idea. When you push your idea, you make me defensive. Selling is a martial art of sorts. In martial arts, we are always looking, patiently, for openings.

If and when you find the right opening—and this takes practice—you then have to be empty and listen. You have to be so empty that you won't even have to take a note. You will concentrate so hard at listening that you will listen and remember. And then your training will connect the features and benefits of your product or service with the prospect's stated dissatisfaction. This is a key reason you need to be so intensely trained on the features and benefits of your product or service. If you are trained, you will introduce these benefits naturally. You will be leading, but your prospects will feel like they are leading. When you behave in this way, your prospects will feel like they are teaching you, and you will be feeling like a student as you sell. This is greatness.

Don't come into a sales call or negotiation with your sword drawn. Come in empty handed; come in formless and shapeless, ready to listen with complete openness until the opportunity to apply your training on your product or service comes. At all times, if you listen hard enough, you will remember all. Don't rush and don't jump the gun. Be patient and be like water to succeed on that next sales call.

The Only Resolution You Need for Next Year

I am a huge fan of Ross Perot. You may think of him as an eccentric billionaire from Texas. You may remember him as the presidential candidate in 1992 when he got 19% of the popular vote (the most for an independent candidate since 1912). Or you may think of him as the small guy with big ears. I think he would be fine with that. Ross Perot succeeded because he has "big ears." He is an incredible listener.

When I think about Ross Perot, I think pure inspiration when it comes to sales or developing a business. He is my icon in that regard. When it comes time for New Year's business-related resolutions, I start and begin with Ross Perot. Why? Young Ross was an IBM salesman after he left the Navy. How did he get that job? While he was an official greeter in the Navy, he met an IBM representative who was impressed with him and told him to look him up after he was discharged, which he was in 1957. And so a young Ross began selling computers for IBM and in 1961, IBM introduced sales quotas. What was Perot's reaction? In 1962, Perot made his annual quota by January 18th. That is what greatness looks like. I live in both Austin and Dallas and I met Perot at a fundraiser. Ross Perot's secret sauce, his special skill, is the only New Year's resolution you need to succeed beyond your wildest dreams: You need to learn to listen and consistently improve your listening skills.

We all think we listen, but we don't. Watch people listen to you. Observe how quickly they respond. Were they listening to you? Maybe they listened for a little bit. Then what happened? Once they formed an opinion of what you were saying, they did what? They began formulating a response. They were responding, not listening. And you can see it in their facial expression. You will note a reaction in their face or bodily gesture at some point while you are talking. They are done listening and they are formulating. Worse yet, interruptions happen all the time in meetings, sales calls, and in random, everyday conversations. But even if you aren't interrupted, your listener's desire to respond detracts from the quality of the listening. What does good listening look like?

I study memory with weekly lessons from Chester Santos, the 2008 Memory Champion. Working with Chester, one thing I learned was that memory and listening are completely interrelated. In trying to improve my memory, I had to become a better listener. I, myself, was a quick responder and reactor—not a listener. I was on a sales negotiation a couple months ago. There were five representatives from the client. I listened so hard I thought I was going to sweat. I withheld my judgment and opinion and just listened. When they finished (and the exchange included a lot of information) I repeated the key elements they wanted at the end, even though they represented different business units with different needs. I hadn't taken a single note. They were astonished and one of them said, "Did you write that on your hand?" Listening is the secret to sales and leadership success, and we got that sale.

As Perot says, "Most people don't listen to customers." His superiors didn't listen to him when he told them what customers wanted. They wanted ancillary services with their computers. What did he do? Built two multi-billion-dollar businesses providing ancillary services.

If you don't believe me, believe Ross Perot. The only New Year's resolution you need to succeed in the future is to dramatically change how well you listen to others. What are some simple exercises you can do to improve your listening skills?

- ***Open your mind and suspend judgment.*** The reason you respond and react instead of listen is because you have an opinion. You agree or you disagree or you think it needs clarifying. Let it be. If you can suspend judgment, you will hear things you haven't heard. Be aware of your "self-talk" and shut it down.
- ***Active listening.*** This doesn't mean repeating word for word what people say to you. It means that after you have listened and after they are done, you give them back the essence in your own words to see if you are connecting.

- ***Never, ever interrupt someone.*** This is the cardinal sin of listening. And it can be so tempting. It tends to happen when you are tired of listening to someone or you greatly disagree. I have seen this on sales calls. It is the kiss of death for a sales team. It shows a complete lack of respect.
- ***To listen properly, get into a meditative state.*** If you don't have a meditative state, you need to get yourself one. As a martial artist, I have one. It is, for me, a mindset of complete focus. In martial arts you need focus or you will get hit. Maybe you can get it from yoga or study it up. But great listening is a martial art!
- ***Check your ego at the door.*** Stop worrying about how smart you are or appear. A lot of bad listening habits come from a desire to show others how smart or right you are. That's good for you, but will be bad for your sales. It ain't about you.
- ***Maintain an encouraging and inviting presence.*** Don't cross your arms. Don't glance around the room. Your facial expression and gestures should reflect openness.
- ***Put down your d*$# PDA!*** I know you imagine that five minutes can't go by without your missing an important email or text. Great listeners never look at their PDAs while they are engaged in a conversation. People who think they are good listeners know it is rude to look at their PDAs. But they can't help themselves. Great listeners resist the PDA temptation.

- ***Pay attention to the facial and bodily gestures of the speaker.*** Take them all in. Why? Studies show that much communication is non-verbal. So listening is tactile. You need to feel it.
- ***Practice, practice, practice.*** Listening is a skill. It is teachable and it is learnable, but there is no substitute for practice. This is the key to continual improvement.
- ***Focus, focus, focus.*** When I am working hard at listening it feels like work! So if it feels like work to improve your listening skills, you are on the right path.

Regardless of what you think of Perot's idiosyncrasies or policies or other opinions, the man was a great listener as a sales person. Even as a presidential candidate he advocated open democracy with electronic town-hall meetings. He has some great quotes, but his simple philosophy is captured by this quote: "Spend a lot of time talking to customers face to face. You'd be amazed how many companies don't listen to their customers." That is still my favorite. It isn't too early to set your New Year's resolutions. I recommend this one, just one, for next year. And check yourself on January 18. Are you done with your annual goals? Don't put on your thinking cap; open your ears and start listening.

The Beauty of Brutal Honesty

I lost another mentor last week, on my birthday, in fact. I turned 56 in Cancun with the help of some Don Julio Reposado tequila, only to learn within hours that our dear friend from the CEO Clubs, Cathy B. Colella, had died. What I knew of Cathy's life came from seeing her three or four times a year over a 15-year period in a Club where we gave each other advice while we travelled to different areas of the world. I knew she had been a Ford Agency model when she was young and had spent time studying at Harvard. By the time I met her she was the owner and CEO of an environmental remediation company in New York City, where she competed with guys who would remind you of the fictional mob boss Tony Soprano.

Cathy had a particular strength and no one was better at it. Cathy was a BS detector and knew how to fearlessly uncover and confront issues and situations with brutal honesty. I am absolutely confident that organizations and people who are honest—brutally honest—with themselves succeed. Organizations and people who live in denial are successful only out of luck. We should all aspire to be more like Cathy and to make sure we try to recruit gems like her to our organizations and lives. Cathy's lesson for me was that brutal honesty can be beautiful. I will miss her, but her voice and face will be with me forever.

My favorite fable as a child was Hans Christian Andersen's "The Emperor's New Clothes." If you haven't read it lately, you owe it to yourself to do so. It is a fable written about the workplace. Two swindlers come to a town where there lives a vain emperor who loves clothes. They convince the emperor to let them sew him a set of clothes and order expensive materials and gold thread to make the clothes, which they simply pocket. These clothes are special. They are invisible to all who are unfit for their jobs. While the clothes are being woven, the emperor sends some of his most trusted counselors to see them. None can, but all report back to the emperor that the clothes are amazing, as they don't want to be unfit for their jobs. Based upon the reports of his counselors, the emperor decides to parade his new clothes through town. The emperor and his minions praise the non-existent clothes. Finally, a young boy watching the parade speaks up and says, "Hey, the emperor has no clothes." Lest you think this is an isolated Danish story, I found versions of this same fable in Turkey, India, Sri Lanka, England and Spain. It is a common fable that with slight variations spans many cultures. In many cultures, the "clothes test" was supposedly to test birth legitimacy.

From a workplace perspective, what is the moral of the story? While there are several, I like to think it is about bad decisions arising from "group think." How does a group collectively make a bad decision that none individually would make? Everyone in the fable knows there are no clothes but they are afraid to say anything because of how they will be perceived—unfit for their jobs. As a result, the leader makes a horrible decision. If you want to be a great contributor to a great organization, you need to listen for self-deception and denial in the workplace, email chatter, and meetings. And when you hear it, you have to be the child (the Cathy Colella) in the room and fearlessly and honestly say, "But wait, the emperor has no clothes."

How can you identify these situations? What phrases, tones and behaviors should you listen for to spot self-deception, denial and bad decision-making in the works? What does it sound like in meetings or company emails or dialogue? Here are some phrases associated with self-denial that I have heard over the years in projects I have led or participated in that did not go well. They would have gone better with engaged, brutal honesty and dialogue.

- ***"It's strategic."*** This can often mean that the numbers, themselves, don't make sense. Using the word "strategic" is designed to hide that fact behind the concept rather than sound financial decision-making.
- ***"They don't get it."*** This is a dismissive phrase to signal you either speak the language or you don't. It is designed to cut off dialogue and debate.
- ***"Don't worry about it. That isn't your concern."*** Generally this means you should worry about it. If you uncover something the organization needs to know about and you

are deeply concerned about it, and someone says this to you, you have to find a way to raise the issue with those who matter.

- ***Any ad-hominem attacks.*** These are attacks on individuals like, "Joe is an idiot and doesn't have a clue." If you hear this, you should consider it a red flag that a topic needs further debate and discussion.
- ***Changing the subject.*** Some people are masterful at this. In workplace discussions and meetings, sometimes you will reach a difficult point in the debate or analysis, then all of a sudden, someone changes the subject. Bring the discussion back to the main area if you can.
- ***Making insignificant distinctions.*** Sometimes you will be in a meeting and find a problem or issue with a proposed course of action or plan. Listen carefully and consider whether the distinctions really matter. I was working on an acquisition when I was young, and the growth rate for the target company seemed too high. When we questioned it, the deal champion said that this was a slightly different segment and would grow faster. It didn't.
- ***Twisting the facts to make them fit the decision.*** If everyone agrees on the facts and you reach an impasse, pay attention carefully if someone tries to rewrite the facts to get past the impasse.
- ***One-sided over-selling.*** If a proposed decision or course of action is overly presented, or only the positives are

presented, this should cause you to dig deeper. A good presentation of a proposed decision should have a balanced view. What are the positives and the negatives?

- ***Use of brute force or politics.*** Listen for language, especially tones, that imply desperation. These are cues that should make your antenna quiver. Politics is the use of indirect means to get approvals that wouldn't be gained if the proper issues were considered.
- ***"It's synergistic—1+1=3."*** This comes up in the context of acquisitions, mergers and combinations. It's not that they aren't conceptually possible; it's just that it generally takes longer and more work for them to materialize, if they do.

You may think you don't have the power or you take a risk in raising a red flag when you encounter behaviors that are designed to prevent good discussion and debate that lead to better decision-making. And there is risk whenever you speak up about such things. Take it. Like the young boy in the fable, Cathy wasn't afraid. And how you react to these behaviors and phrases really matters. What was special about Cathy is that when she told me or anyone else the brutal truth, she didn't beat you with it. She just said it like it was the most natural thing in the world. Similar to the young boy in the fable, she just gave you what you needed to hear in a matter-of-fact way. In one particular situation she said to me, "You have fire in your belly but you need to have blood in your mouth." I know that sounds strange, but what she was telling me was that I needed to have stronger execution in the conflict I was in, not just a tough and bold attitude. At one meeting (we may have been in Iceland) she said, "I am going to come to your daughter's graduation." We were all having a good time so I didn't think much of it. On graduation day, she flew from New York to St. Louis and attended my daughter's graduation. She just showed up. I acted surprised and she simply said, "I said I would do it." That whole experience was in some way designed to get me to a higher "say/do" ratio.

Approach the input you provide to your organization with childlike innocence, not know-it-all aggression. If your organization doesn't want to hear your innocent questions when you speak up about behaviors that hinder sound organizational decision-making, you may need a new organization. Great companies and great leaders welcome robust and honest debate and the input of all. Listen, listen, and listen for behaviors, tones, and words that are designed to derail good decision-making processes. Having said that, if after they take in all the input they decide to go left and you think they should go right, you need to support left and support corporate functionality and discipline.

I, along with many, will miss the beautiful, brutally honest Cathy Colella. I suspect she is somewhere now, watching a parade, listening to the folks compliment the non-existent clothes, shaking her head and preparing to lovingly and yet firmly tell the emperor he needs to put on some clothes.

RE-CAP: WHITE BELT LISTENING TECHNIQUES

- ***Decide to become a good listener.*** Commit to training yourself to listen. Commit to an end-of-day self-exam: How did I do at listening today? What worked and what didn't? Begin your day with an affirmation that includes listening.
- ***Eliminate distraction and temptation.*** Put your PDA in your pocket or purse or someplace you can't see it or feel it.
- ***"Look Eye," as Mr. Miagi said to the Karate Kid.*** Look at the person speaking with you. Look at the face, but take in everything. Remember that most communication is non-verbal.
- ***Drop your sword.*** Learn to defend. Learn not to always throw the first punch or say the first words.
- ***Appear open.*** Adopt postures that are welcoming, i.e., don't cross your arms. Be ready to listen and look ready.
- ***Encourage.*** Smile and nod to make the speaker feel good and comfortable.

BLUE BELT

PRACTICAL TECHNIQUES FOR EXCHANGES

White belts are just beginning and very quickly learn they know too little to exchange with others. They respect how little they know and how much there is to know. Blue belts start to learn practical techniques that can lead them to victory in matches, and begin to have the confidence to try these techniques. The three essays that follow contain three invaluable listening-related skills. The first essay, "No Notes: How to Listen and Remember Every Meeting and Sales Call," provides invaluable observations and techniques to help you remember what people say or have said without the distraction of trying to simultaneously take notes. Some of it is based on martial arts experience and some is based on my memory training.

In most traditional academic training and job-skills training, the right brain is neglected. The right brain has a higher IQ than the left brain, and needs to get in the game. Martial arts engages both sides of the brain as well as motor memory. The second essay, "Listening for Rhythm to Negotiate and Sell," teaches that your speaker—in martial arts, your opponent—has a rhythm and that sales and negotiations have rhythms. As a blue belt, you begin to be aware of these rhythms, and more important, you learn you can affect these rhythms. Finally, the third essay, "Embracing the Power of Silence in Sales," introduces one of the most powerful concepts in listening: the power of silence. Masterful martial artists and masterful salespeople, negotiators and leaders use silence like an invisible light sabre. As a blue belt you are introduced to these concepts.

No Notes: How to Listen and Remember Every Meeting and Sales Call

When I was young, there were no Xerox machines. We did have carbon copies, though. Why my friends from grade school are still alive and have not succumbed to carbon or ink poisoning is a miracle. As we sat in Atlantic Avenue elementary school in Pittsburgh at our wooden desks, I remember our teacher would hand out purple-ink pages from the mimeograph machine and we would take a deep breath and smell the ink on the paper before handing it back to the kid in the desk behind us. And they would snort the ink-covered paper and pass it back to the next kid, and so on. I can remember that smell to this day—it stunk up the whole room. I also remember my eyes watering if I got a good enough whiff. We would breathe out, then breathe in with our noses tight to the paper, breathing in as long as we could. With all the things in those chemicals that are bad for you, I am surprised I haven't had any health consequences, but there is still time, I suppose.

As you go through your business life, especially meetings and sales calls, you will often find yourself wishing you had an invisible Xerox machine so you could truly listen and not have to take notes. As you probably have noticed, taking notes is actually a distraction from listening. You have to look down to write, away from the speakers or audiences who are your buyers.

I am fascinated by jobs, job skills and improvement. The fundamentals with respect to the workplace are critical to getting you to the next level. I am somewhat of a "polymath." The word has nothing to do with math; it simply means you are more like a Renaissance person than a technical specialist. I suppose this comes from a career in which I was in-house lawyer for a large company, outside counsel (associate and partner) in a large law firm, an entrepreneur and founder of small businesses, executive in a big company, a writer, and a martial artist. And beyond that, I have lived in 10 different states. While I don't necessarily recommend this life to everyone, the diversity has given me a unique perspective on life, progress, careers, success and failure. I write to share these unique perspectives, not because I have done everything perfectly or even well, but because I have tried more things more ways, and in more places. And perhaps my experiences can help others skip some steps, especially the ones I wish I would have skipped. This essay is about walking and chewing gum, listening and remembering, and walking away from a client or meeting with a photographic image in your head of what happened and what you need to do. It is designed to help you remember as if you have a Xerox machine inside your ear.

Most people try to take notes as they sit in a sales call or in a meeting. In a modern meeting, you may take notes by hand on a piece of paper, by typing directly into your laptop, by scribbling on a modern electronic pad, or some combination of the above. I have tried all these note-taking methods, and each time I found that while I was transcribing, I was often missing something else. Meetings and sales calls are not like a class in school. At school you are being presented with information with the understanding that you will take notes during the lecture. Good professors will even watch as the class takes notes, and time their cadence to the rhythm of those who are following along. Good luck with this on a sales call. Just when you are about to write something down, several things will be mentioned that you will miss.

Of all my polymath endeavors, I like selling the best. I have sold legal services, transportation services, logistics services, human resource services, staffing, recruiting, jobs and real estate, to name a few. I have been on hundreds of sales calls with some of the largest and smallest companies in America. I love to sell. Selling is about changing behavior. You can't change behavior if people don't respect you. And if you can get them to admire you, they will—or are much more likely to—buy from you. Selling is still an emotional experience between buyer and seller, no matter how technical the underlying product or service. One of the best ways to have someone admire you is to have superior listening and remembering skills and use them during the sales call. This is not just because it is cool; it also allows you to use professional selling techniques, because if you remember all of their pain points or challenges and opportunities, you can introduce the benefits of your service or product seamlessly into the conversation.

I no longer take notes *during* a sales meeting or any other meeting; I do write them down afterwards. And while it took me some time to develop this skill, you can do it too. Here are some of my techniques:

- ***Active listening that translates needs into your industry jargon.*** When you hear something important, you need to repeat it, not in the same words, but capturing the same meaning. And when you do this, use words that you will remember. Example: Suppose you are selling staffing services. The prospect says, "We need our jobs filled within 3 days." You say, "Okay, I got it, your SLA for time to fill is 72 hours." "SLA," "time to fill," and the hours are all language from staffing that you are more likely to remember. You have not only understood their requirements, you have also shown you know what you are doing. Now all you really have to remember is 72 hours. The rest will come to you.
- ***Know who you are meeting and who they are.*** Use LinkedIn and don't be one of those creepy anonymous stalkers. I use LinkedIn and I am not one of those stalkers. If I visit your profile, you will know I went there—and I want you to know. I want you to know I care who you are. You should be respected for doing your homework. If someone comes

to meet me and doesn't check me out on LinkedIn, I respect them less. If they tell me they checked on LinkedIn and did it anonymously, I hate that. What are you trying to hide? The better you know the players, the more likely you will remember what they say because you can associate what they say with who they are.

- ***You must memorize the roles of those you're meeting with before the meeting.*** If you go into a sales call and don't know the names, background and organizational roles of those you are trying to sell, shame on you. You'd better take notes because my techniques won't help you. You are entitled to know who will be in the meeting and what role they play, and you need to do your research on them. Knowing their role is absolutely critical because you have to communicate very differently based on their role. Example: Suppose you are selling billing services. And suppose there is a procurement representative, a CFO, a CIO and an accounts receivable clerk. The procurement person cares about price; the CFO cares about functionality, price, compatibility and scalability; the CIO cares about system integrity and software compatibility, and the A/R clerk cares about functionality. Work to sell the A/R clerk on price? They couldn't care less. Try to sell the procurement person on the great features and it'll fall on deaf ears. If you know the roles, you will remember who says what because the things they say are predictable based on their roles in the organization. Someone who has responsibility for budgets is very different than someone who needs to buy something to make their work easier.

- ***Study the room and players as you walk in and notice any unique features.*** You can then associate these unique features with a point you want to remember. Suppose there is a conference phone and it has a unique shape. You can actually visualize the phone and store points on each side of the phone for remembering later. Or suppose the leader of the meeting is wearing purple. Use it to remember something. This integrates your right brain into the meeting. I must confess that I use the services of a memory coach, Chester Santos (www.chestersantos.com), and I recommend that you study memorization. It is an invaluable skill. Right-brain techniques are powerful tools that with a little training and practice can set you apart.

- ***Create a story out of the needs of the customer.*** Stories are easier to remember than lists. Use your right brain to create a story about the need, challenge or opportunity of the prospect. Example: Suppose you are selling radio advertising and having trouble because the prospect tried radio advertising once, spent a bunch of money, and got no new sales. You might imagine a van bearing the company's name, and a radio antenna on top of the van spewing dollar bills into the street. They go straight into the gutter. Again, this is a right-brain technique that will help you remember the problem and challenge associated with your prospect.

We can't carry a Xerox machine into a sales meeting or other important business event. Listening and remembering is a hallmark of greatness. Work on your listening skills and translate customer needs into jargon you remember as a form of active listening. Know the names, personalities and roles of those with whom you will engage. Get your right brain into the game to blow away your buyers with your keen focus and photographic memory. If you feel the need to have a pencil and paper in front of you to show respect, you can do that, but your listening will be better if you don't look down to make a note. I have tried this no-notes technique in several key sales to very large companies. In each case, the prospects asked me how I remembered everything they said when I summarized at the end. I simply said, "I listened. We listen."

Good luck and go get 'em.

Listening for Rhythm to Negotiate and Sell

We spend a lot of time teaching content in sales and negotiation settings. I went through what was referred to as the Professional Selling System when I was at Union Pacific Railroad in the mid '80s (this was based on "needs-based" selling strategy). And as a lawyer I have been to many negotiation seminars based on the book *Getting to Yes.* These are excellent programs, but based on my 31-plus years of work in the field, I think we aren't teaching and learning enough about what in the end differentiates the closers and the folks that get deals done on their terms. We sometimes refer to this intangible element as instinct or timing or charisma. It carries the emblem of alchemy. It is the part of sales and negotiation that engineers and technical people sometimes find hard to understand. Some think it un-teachable. But it is teachable. Great negotiators have strong technical skills and training, but what they also do well is listen carefully and get in touch with the rhythm of the person or people on the other side. They are in touch with the back-and-forth, like black belts in human exchange.

Face-to-face sales or negotiation is a like a dance, a fight, an operatic exchange. Points and counterpoints are exchanges of words and also emotion. I am not going to try to convince you that there is a rhythm to human exchanges. If you don't believe me, stick with what you are doing. If you want to test what I am talking about, try some of my tactics below.

Have a conversation with a friend or significant other. Say something you know they will disagree with. What do you get? They will likely argue with you, picking up the pace in the process. Saying something controversial tends to turn up the heat and get things moving faster. Want to slow things down? Say something obvious or repetitive. Try this. If someone goes silent on you, they may have advanced skills, which I will describe in a moment. But in general, you can change the tempo of a face-to-face exchange simply by deciding whether to say something controversial or something obvious.

Specifically in a sales or negotiation context, if you are not making progress and getting lots of objections, you are not going to advance your cause by arguing. You need to back off and slow down. Say something obvious that no one can disagree with to regain your footing. And notice that this is consistent with the technical side of need-satisfaction sales. If you are having trouble closing, you need to remind your prospects of the benefits they have already accepted.

To listen well in a conversation, you can't just listen to the words and you can't just watch the body language and intonation. You need to listen for, feel, and get in sync with the rhythm. Are you in a waltz? A techno-dance? A tango? Find some art you really understand that has different rhythms. Everyone you sit across from has a natural rhythm they have developed. Gain an advantage by figuring out what it is. As a martial artist, I use slow rhythms like tai chi and fast rhythms like karate to describe in my mind the virtual human movement I am feeling in sales or negotiating. For my own personal style, I really love using a Jiu Jitsu rhythm for sales because it is a gentle martial art that involves thinking about what someone is going to do next, and feeling them before they move. It has a wonderful flow to it. Maybe you love music. Use the different music rhythms to keep you in touch.

And now, back to silence. Silence is truly golden when it comes to sales and negotiation. What is my best tip for handling silence if you are trying to sell or trying to get a point in negotiation? Be quiet yourself. Respond in kind. Whoever speaks first after that, loses. In our noisy world today, we have lost the gift of silence. Those who practice silence are like modern Jedi Knights, practicing a long-lost martial art. In the Russian Martial Art we spend lots of time being quiet and relaxing so we can feel others, not ourselves.

There is one sure-fire way to lose touch with the rhythm of a human exchange. That is to bring stress to the situation. If you enter an exchange with stress, you will never feel the rhythm of the other people. All you will feel is yourself.

Winners respect rhythm and know how to sense it and change it up. Pay attention to the rhythm of your exchanges with other humans, and learn how to use rhythm to redirect and win sales and negotiations.

Embracing the Power of Silence in Sales

I have been on too many sales calls in my lifetime where there is a gap or a quiet point, and a salesperson jumps in to fill it. Whether I am the buyer or part of a sales team including the salesperson, I always cringe. It is hard to watch. It is hard to listen to and observe. For me, it is akin to someone scratching fingernails on a chalkboard. I want to scream, but can't. I want to say, "Shut up and let the prospect absorb and think." But that would be interrupting and come off worse. Never, ever disrespect the value and power of silence in a sales or negotiation scenario. Learn to respect the power of silence in all human exchange.

Selling is about getting people to change their behavior. Regardless of all the math and financial ROIs that go into it, changing behavior involves emotions. If it didn't, we wouldn't need sales people. But we do. Human change is a human process involving subtle cues and deeply human exchanges. I have listened to and watched prospects make buying decisions for over 30 years in every context you can imagine. There is a look I have come to recognize when they decide, even if they don't tell you. We are all looking for this. We call them buying signals. Do you know the ultimate buying signal from a prospect? Silence. In that moment of silence they are imagining buying from you. They are imagining what they will tell their existing supplier. They are imagining what they will tell their peers or their boss or procurement.

The world seems to contain an overabundance of noise and advice. Consider the fundamental law of supply and demand. The supply and demand curves tell us that as supply goes up, if demand stays the same, price goes down. This is a fundamental law of microeconomics. And sure enough, advice these days (including the millions of blogs and LinkedIn Posts) is free. So economics is working. It is noisy out there. So if it is noisy out there, what is in short supply? Silence.

People pay for meditation, yoga, and trips to the woods or mountains—any place to get away from the noise. I have lived in downtown high rises in major cities. Silence? Between sirens, motorcycles, construction, dogs barking and neighbors, it is a noisy world. And it is not just about having quiet time for sleep. Daytime silence is important as well. The workplace itself has become much noisier, in my opinion. I understand the value of open-door policies and always being accessible. But when do you get to think? So many great thoughts, ideas and inventions have come during periods of meditation or daydreaming. Whether Newton was hit in the head or not with an apple, by contemporaneous accounts, he was actually daydreaming in the garden the day he "discovered" gravity. Silence is a cool and productive state. It is a state wherein we concentrate, think, contemplate and invent.

Remember the last time you were in deep thought and a noise interrupted it. Or maybe someone interrupted you and you lost your train of thought. What did you think of that thing or person that so rudely interrupted your blessed silence? Your self-talk turned to hatred and you said, “Why can’t they shut that dog up?” Or you said, “Do we really have to do the dishes right now?” Or maybe you said, “You interrupted me and now I can’t remember what I was going to say.” Imagine what your prospects think of you when you interrupt their thinking.

How hard is it to find a great prospect? How many emails do you have to send to get a phone contact? How many phone contacts do you have to make to get a face-to-face call? How many meetings do you need to have to get the actual decision-maker in the room? After all that work, you decide to interrupt the silence?

Say less and listen more on sales calls. It is that simple. As your prospect or decision-maker is listening to you and pondering, when you are done, be done. Let them have their time. They are studying you and what you said. Sit back and relax and wait. If you have the patience, you will see that buying signal. It will first be manifested in body language, not words. You may see their eyes look off into the distance; you may see them stare at your ROI model or other handout. And while they do that don’t become a bad Ronco commercial—"Hey wait, there is more.” Be still. Be quiet. Worship the silence that is there.

For me, I find it helpful to let the song "*Sounds of Silence,*" by Simon and Garfunkel, drift through my mind (some of my favorite lyrics are below). Or you can imagine a peaceful place that you love. I like to think of Lake Tahoe or the old cemetery that sits on the hillside on the road to Cortona, Italy. If the references to Ronco commercials and Simon and Garfunkel are lost on you, look them up. They will help you communicate with us 78-million Baby Boomers. Hush now, and go sell something!

And in the naked light I saw
Ten thousand people, maybe more.
People talking without speaking,
People hearing without listening,
People writing songs that voices never share
And no one dared
Disturb the sound of silence.

RE-CAP: BLUE BELT LISTENING TECHNIQUES

- ***Active listening.*** After someone makes a point, without interrupting, try to interpret what they are saying in your own words and gain their assent before they move to the next topic.
- ***Be aware of differences between tone and the meaning of the words themselves.*** E.g., they say, "Don't worry, it is water under the bridge." But their tone says they are still angry. This is when body language tells you more about their intent than the words.
- ***Ego.*** Check your ego at the door. If it is all about you, you won't learn from anyone else.
- ***Bite your tongue.*** Prevent yourself from interrupting. Listen to others as they interrupt, and fight the temptation to interrupt back.
- ***Meditative state.*** Begin to develop your meditative state. Learn to empty yourself. Clean your mind of bias.
- ***Relax.*** Become aware of your breathing and breathe in through your nose and out through your mouth. Let your breathing relax you.

PURPLE BELT

ADVANCING THE SKILLS OF MOVEMENT AND ATTENTION

The next three essays help you move better in conversation. They are about understanding choices in your listening engagements and influencing others through those choices. "*Learning to Pivot from No*" is an essay about asking and listening instead of running over and through others. Based on the popular childhood book *Green Eggs and Ham*, it shows the difference between asking and listening and telling. "*Say This, Not That*" is about wise word selection when you are listening. It is about removing ego from the listening equation. Mind drift is another inevitable part of being human and something we all need to be sensitive to in our daily living. It is why we often don't hear our significant others or spouses. "What Did You Just Say?" helps us be aware of and deal with mind drift. As a purple belt, you are ready to learn to be honest when your mind drifts, make better word selections when you respond to someone in a conversation and learn the value of asking and listening, not telling.

Learning to Pivot from "No!"

What is the first word you remember? It might be "no." And the word "no" is etched deeply in our psyches as something to fear. The source of the fear arises from the classical conditioning that accompanies the spoken word, "no." When we are young, "no" can accompany a slap, a spanking, a nasty expression from a parent or teacher, being deprived of an object and perhaps a strong negative tone. "No" is a powerful word and a word worthy of some reflection if you have any involvement in sales or negotiation. What is the role of "no," and how can we learn to not fear it and not ignore it? How can we listen and ask about it, and through that understanding, achieve our goals?

If you had a good childhood, your family had Dr. Seuss books on some bookshelves somewhere. Maybe you enjoyed *The Cat in the Hat.* Perhaps you liked *Hop on Pop.* My favorite was, and will always be, *Green Eggs and Ham.* I may not have recognized it as a book about sales then, even though I was a salesman myself. I would get up early every morning and deliver the *Pittsburgh Post-Gazette* at 5:30 am before school. At the tender age of 11, I was a door-to-door salesman, pushing the Sunday and holiday editions of the paper and seeking to expand my route.

But I surely see Sam-I-Am as a salesman now. And I am not the only one who has recognized this parallel. Some sales folks view the story as about the reward that finally comes with persistence, because eventually, the green eggs and ham are eaten and enjoyed by the target. And the sale occurs with only 50 words repeated endlessly, part of a bet between Seuss and his publisher that he couldn't write a book with fewer than 236 words *(The Cat in The Hat).*

But Sam-I-Am is a lousy listener, simply pushing his product, green eggs and ham, over and over again in different ways, until wanting to never hear from Sam again, the target says, "Sam! If you let me be, I will try them. You will see." This comes after being offered them here or there, with a mouse, in a house, with a fox, in a box, on a train, in a car, in a tree, and in the dark. It is a great read and is consistently ranked as one of the top children's books of all time. But Green Eggs and Ham is a lousy lesson in listening, sales and negotiation. Not once does Sam-I-Am ask the simple question, "What don't you like about green eggs and ham?" Not once is there any effort on the part of Sam-I-Am to ask and listen. Instead, his response to rejection is simply another pitch.

As I reflect on my childhood sales experiences, I actually think I modeled Sam-I-Am. I remember being called persistent and having doors closed in my face trying to sell holiday editions of the *Pittsburgh Post-Gazette.* We were supposed to use the holiday editions to try and get regular subscribers for the daily newspaper. It is sad that door-to-door selling doesn't exist much anymore. It was a great training ground.

But imagine if Sam-I-Am had asked questions instead of just pushing until the target wants you off his or her porch?

I think it would be a fun project to rewrite *Green Eggs and Ham* and recast Sam-I-Am, so that when he first asks, "Do you like green eggs and ham?" and the prospect says, "I do not like them, Sam-I-Am, I do not like green eggs and ham," Sam-I-Am listened and said, "You do not like green eggs and ham? Which is the worst, green eggs or ham?" Showing the character trying to learn more about the tastes and preferences and desires of the customer would make a great children's book.

We need to unlearn our fear of "no," but not ignore it either. "No" can be the beginning of great sales. In the end, Sam-I-Am sold a seemingly strange and hard-to-sell product with persistence. Some view it as a success, and kids, as I did when I was young, love it. But as far as a lesson in listening, the book is a perfect example of what not to do. "No" needs to lead to questions to discover what the objection is. Get good at pivoting off "no" and you, too, can sell green eggs and ham. It may not even take you 50 words, because you should be asking and listening and talking less. My favorite childhood book may hold clues as to why at 56 I am spending the whole year trying to become a better listener.

Say This, Not That

When I was young, only my Italian friends' families used olive oil. In upstate New York virtually all of my friends were from families of Italian descent, so I got to taste olive oil and eat it a lot on bread and pizza. In my Welsh, German, Slavic/ Russian household with dairy farming roots, we used butter for almost everything. When butter wasn't appropriate, we used mayonnaise—homemade mayonnaise from real eggs. Now, there are lots of websites and books that teach you to "eat this, not that." Instead of tuna fish salad, you eat turkey, thereby avoiding mayonnaise. Instead of margarine or butter, you use olive oil. "Eat this, not that" promises that you will lose weight if you substitute one food for another. For example, Cocoa Puffs are ok but Cocoa Pebbles are not. Substituting one food for a similar food is easier than dieting because you are just trading one similar thing for another, but the substitute has far fewer calories. Bad listening habits, like bad eating habits, are also more easily corrected with substitutions: Eat this, not that; say this, not that.

Like eating, talking and listening are basic, rudimentary life skills and essential elements of the workplace. They lead (or not) to communication, which is the basis of getting things done together. Communication is one of the building blocks of any team's progress, and the extent to which team members communicate efficiently and effectively often determines team success.

There are many responsive phrases that are "show stoppers" and impose impediments to the progress of communication. Show-stopping phrases tend to introduce ego and emotion into communication. Avoiding these phrases and replacing them with others is a simple way to accelerate progress in communicating and accomplishing together.

As we listen to someone, we all, unknowingly and unintentionally, introduce phrases that aren't constructive, but make us feel better. And these phrases are destructive. Here are some examples of destructive responses that halt a conversation, and some alternate phrases (say this, not that) that make communication more efficient and effective. Like improving your eating with "eat this, not that," you can improve your listening with "say this, not that."

- ***"Relax" or "Calm down."*** When conversations get heated and we are listening to someone rant or speak heatedly, we may be tempted to say, "Relax" or "Calm down." This never works and tends to amplify emotions. The speaker thinks that you are criticizing them for being overly emotional. So, instead, say nothing and let them run their course. If you want to say anything, say, "I understand."
- ***"You don't get it."*** This is more common in tech circles. When I was in the Bay Area in the '90s there were two kinds of people, if you listened to the nomenclature

of the day. "They don't get it." This meant they didn't understand, for example, that revenue didn't matter when it came to dot coms. Instead, say, "Hey, I did a bad job explaining my point. Let me try again." Telling someone they don't get it is immediately combative.

- ***"That's what I said."*** So what? This is just your ego talking. Why not just say, "I agree." Or you could say, "Great idea." If you said it and they say the same thing, what difference does it make to team progress whose idea it was? It is just an ego battle over credit, which adds nothing to the communication except tension.
- ***"You're not listening."*** Anything that is explicitly or implicitly critical will get in the way of communication progress. If you don't feel they are getting your point, try, "Let me put this a different way."
- ***"Actually."*** This is a personal pet peeve. When you are listening to someone and then say, "actually," you are correcting by sounding superior. It is an insult with a huge dose of ego on top. How about trying, "I was thinking" or "I was wondering."
- ***"I know" or "I thought of that."*** If you know, good. But keep it to yourself if you want to make progress in a communication. "I know" is the opposite of "actually." "I know" is defensive in nature. To make progress in a conversation say, "What should we do about that?" instead of "I know."

- ***"Of course."*** This phrase tells speakers they are saying the obvious and makes them feel stupid. Say, "I agree" instead. "I agree" reinforces and advances the conversation. "Of course" introduces ego and one-upmanship.

"Say this, not that" phrases are designed to reduce ego and tension in conversation and communication. As a listener, you will help conversations and communications progress by avoiding phrases and words that cause shields to go up and people to get angry or defensive. Team progress and ultimately your progress in an organization will be based in large part on how well you listen. How you respond when you are listening and learning to use phrases that make team communication more efficient and effective is critical to your advancement. Say this, not that.

What Did You Just Say?

You know the feeling. You have felt it. It is a sinking feeling followed by panic. Someone is talking to you and your mind drifts. And now they say, "What do you think?" And you think, but don't say, "About what?" Yikes! Whether you are distracted by a Laguna Beach sunset, your own thoughts on the subject being discussed, or just plain bored, drifting happens. Let's face it. It's challenging to completely quiet your mind. Why? Because the human mind has been designed and evolved to be "ready." A ready mind is active and active minds tend to wander. Imagine what our ancestors would have become if they'd had a quiet mind in the middle of the Savannah. The answer? Dinner. How should we handle it when we drift in the middle of a conversation and what are some tips to reduce "drift"?

If you "wake up" in the middle of a conversation, the most emotionally intelligent thing to do is tell the truth. Stop the speaker and say, "I am so sorry, my mind drifted. Here is the last thing I remember." There may be temporary disappointment or rebuke for your mind drift, depending upon the relationship, but you will find that honesty about mind drift is the best strategy in dealing with the speaker you neglected. If the speaker wants to know what you were thinking about, you may not know. Minds don't ask for permission when they drift. I tend to say that my mother popped into my head when I don't know why I drifted. Why not? Many of our habits, including listening, are formed in early childhood. I suppose I will know how many folks read this essay if someone I talk to says to me, "Sorry, my mind drifted. I was thinking about my mother." It would be fun if that came back to me. Someone drifts while I am talking. I notice and say, "Hey, you okay?" and the person responds, "Sorry, I was thinking about my mother."

What about the flip side of the drifting issue? Suppose you are talking and someone you are speaking to gazes off into the distance or otherwise disengages. This one is easy. Just stop talking. Wait. Both as a listener and a talker you need to pay attention to the body language of those you are with. A 1971 study said that 55% of communication is body language. This is especially true when tone and body language diverge. The most important body language with respect to paying attention involves the eyes. You can train yourself to tell whether someone has drifted away from you. Watch their eyes. As Mr. Miagi said to the Karate Kid, "Look Eye." If their eyes look away, they are drifting. When their eyes look away, just stop talking. They will likely look at you and then you can start talking again. Try it.

Mind drift is a real detriment to listening. So here are some techniques to reduce your drifting tendencies.

- ***Keep your eyes on the speaker's face.*** If your eyes move, your mind wanders. Think about it. If you want to change your mind, you change your gaze. So keep your eyes focused and your mind is more likely to stay focused.

- ***Pocket your device.*** We have modern distractions. When I was young we didn't worry about who was trying to tweet, text, email or call us. Nowadays, if you can see or even feel your device, it triggers you to check it. Try and hold your PDA for an hour without checking to see who is "pinging" you one way or another.

- ***Breathe and be aware of your tension.*** If you come into a conversation with tension, even unrelated to the speaker, you will not get much out of it. Tension draws you inward and by definition you are less receptive to someone else. How to reduce tension? In the Russian Martial Art we use breathing and segmented tension techniques to be aware of and eliminate tension. In basic terms, you isolate and tense various muscles while you breathe in, and relax them as you breathe out. This helps you be aware of, and eliminate tension.

- ***Embrace the tone of the speaker.*** Enjoy the tone and tempo of speech of the person with whom you are engaged. This will help you focus. The same 1971 study that said body language was 55% of communication found that voice tone was 38%. Everyone has a unique tone and tempo. Enjoy the differences.

- ***Don't zombie-listen.*** While you should empty yourself of tension and your own thoughts in order to focus on those speaking to you, don't freeze or act unnatural. Get engaged with your speaker and let your body language flow with the conversation. Nod to reinforce things you agree with and withhold where you disagree. To listen well you should not interrupt, but instead influence with your body language.

One of the most embarrassing interpersonal situations is to be caught ignoring someone who is earnestly trying to convey something to you. Our active minds drift. You can reduce the likelihood of mind drift by staying physically engaged, focused, and tension-free, and engaging with the speaker physically. And if someone drifts on you, just stop talking. A great conversation is like a dance—rhythmic and fun. Remember the importance of body language and tone. If you add the role of body language (55%) and tone (38%), and subtract from 100%, you arrive at the shocking conclusion of the 1971 study: Only 7% of communication involves the actual words themselves. (Note: The above percentages were found to be most true when there was a divergence in tone and meaning.)

RE-CAP: PURPLE BELT LISTENING TECHNIQUES

- ***Know your speaker.*** Study people you are going to meet with in advance. Look at pictures of them. Read about them.

- ***Absorb details and unique features.*** When you meet those with whom you will be conversing, study their unique features. People telegraph so much about themselves, but we aren't "listening." You can use unique features to remember names. This is what memory experts do—they study faces.
- ***Right-brain retention.*** As you listen, create stories around points that speakers make. The stranger you make the stories, the more you will remember what they said and the points they made.
- ***Rhythm.*** Relax and feel the rhythm of a conversation, sale or negotiation. Feel the music and dance of it. Sometimes dialogue moves fast and sometimes slow.
- ***Tension.*** Relax so you can feel the tension of the other person. If you are tense, you cannot feel it. Use segmented tension and breathing exercises to be aware of and remove your tension.
- ***Harmony and disharmony.*** Respond in kind to progress towards harmony when conversations go south. Disagree to bring disruption and chaos to a conversation. Practice moving back and forth so you can help someone speak to you.

BROWN BELT

MASTERING SPECIAL SITUATIONS AND THE ROOT CAUSES OF INTERRUPTIONS

As you progress in belt rankings you begin to learn to deal with specialized scenarios. In physical martial arts you may now be learning techniques for dealing with weapons or someone of superior size or power. And so we begin to consider how to listen to bosses, especially when they are angry, in "How to Listen to Your Angry Boss." We also learn the difference between communicating with introverts and extraverts and how to listen to each (they require very different skills and approaches) in "Frosty, The Taz and Learning to Listen to Introverts." But first, we go deeper into the evils of interruptions and consider the root causes of the destructive conversations that arise from cycles of interruptions in "I Am Sorry to Interrupt You, But..."

I Am Sorry to Interrupt You, But...

I like the simple changes that make a big difference in our day-to-day lives. Take the ketchup bottle for example. When I was a lad, ketchup was packaged in glass bottles. Having watched a "bottling run" on a field trip to H. J. Heinz when I was in elementary school in Pittsburgh, I can tell you the ketchup went in the bottle easier than it came out. In fact, getting the ketchup out of the bottle was a physical challenge. You had to bang and bang on the bottom of the bottle just to get that thick ketchup moving. And once you did get it moving, you inevitably got too much. It was a real problem as your hamburger or hot dog got cold waiting and watching for the ketchup to move. Now, the bottles are upside down from how they were in my Wonder Bread years, and you squeeze just the right amount onto your burger or hot dog.

In my day, ketchup makers liked to brag about how thick and consequently slow their ketchup was. Talk about a "bottle neck." Everyone hated it as they struggled to get ketchup out of the bottle. Heinz even ran a set of commercials to brag about the thickness of their ketchup, and to try to turn the "bottle neck" into a plus. Based on Carly Simon's song, "Anticipation," the ad showed a couple of kids waiting for their ketchup to move out of the bottle and portrayed them as excited about the wait. "Thick Heinz Ketchup, the taste that is worth the wait."

Waiting for that ketchup took patience—a Herculean challenge for a pre-teen with the smell of a juicy, freshly cooked cheeseburger in front of him. Properly participating in a good conversation takes that same patience. What happens when we become impatient? We interrupt the speakers—those who are trying to express themselves. If I had to pick the worst listening habit, especially between those who work together or are in a more intimate relationship, it is interrupting one another. What is the cost of dysfunctional communication? There is no telling. And the result? Sub-optimal performance in a team, and emotional side effects and scars that lead to even worse performance. In a relationship? You tell me how long your partner remembers the last time you interrupted them.

So how can you stop, or at least reduce, your tendency to interrupt others? It happens so fast. And what do interrupters, including myself, say? "I'm sorry, I didn't mean to interrupt." Or, "I am sorry to interrupt, but..." Think about those phrases. Of course you didn't "mean" to interrupt, but you did. And are you really sorry to interrupt? You may be sorry to have to do it, but not sorry you did it. So interrupting is an involuntary act? It happens so fast, doesn't it? If you want to interrupt less, you have to understand the root causes of interrupting, and that interrupting someone comes at the end of a process.

Here are some of the root causes of the interrupting process, and how to prevent or reduce the likelihood they will happen.

- ***The slow talker.*** You recognize this interruption scenario. You are listening to someone and it just isn't going fast enough, and you have to pound the bottom of that ketchup bottle to get them talking faster. Don't try to nudge them along. The person could be an introvert. Breathe and give them the time to develop and express their thoughts. Remember the tortoise and the hare. This person may be the tortoise. And when you engage them, slow down yourself. This is a very effective sales and communication strategy: matching speech patterns.

- ***The "I already know what you are going to say."*** This interruption is common in interpersonal relationships, especially long-term relationships. You presume what your partner is going to say based on years of interactions. Stop presuming that you know where someone's thoughts are headed. Thoughts are actually very personal. Calm and empty your mind of preconceptions. Listen openly.

- ***The pointless speech***. Think John Candy in *Planes, Trains and Automobiles.* This is talking that seemingly has no point and when it is done, nobody quite knows what to say. If there is a group, they will all look around at each other and look dumbfounded. Try some body language for this talker. You might look at your watch; fidget. Most communication is non-verbal. Work that.

- ***The conversation "Dominator."*** This is the person who is constantly interrupting others and dominating the conversation. Taking on this person leads to a conversational brawl. Only one way to prevent this. Avoid Dominators. But what if they are on your team or a team leader? Find a time outside of the conversation to discuss this issue with the Dominator. If the person doesn't care, see "group think," below. Or set it up so his or her boss can see the person in action as a Dominator. If the Dominator's boss is a Dominator? You may need a new job.

- ***The "You are wrong."*** This interrupter disagrees with you so needs to correct you, and the sooner the better. This is a mistake. If you interrupt people you disagree with, you may end up with a "group-think" level of decision-making. In other words, you are so set in your ways and opinion that you lose the possibility—no matter how slight you think that is—of learning something. Go read some articles about "group think," like the classic *Harvard Business Review* case regarding the failed Bay of Pigs invasion.
- ***The "You are stupid; I am superior to you."*** These interrupters think they are smarter, more successful, have higher social status and are better looking than everyone else. They feel entitled to interrupt all those they feel superior to in some respect. If you are this person, your "superiority" will be short lived. Eventually, nobody will listen to you. Get some humility in your diet by hanging around people who are smarter, more successful, have higher social status or are better looking than you. If you

can't find someone superior to yourself, you have serious problems that may require professional assistance.

- ***The repeater.*** This is the person who seems to repeat things that have already been said. You have already heard the point being made, so who needs it? Right? When repeaters say something that has already been said, they could be practicing active listening themselves. They may only be understanding it or absorbing it for the first time. People absorb ideas at such different rates and in such different ways. Some folks think conceptually and they get it fast. Other folks are engineers who need to see the bricks in place more than once. Is one listening style or speed better than the other? Of course not. Once engineers "see the bricks," they tend to have a deeper understanding than the fast-moving, conceptual thinker.

What if you are the person who seems to get interrupted? If this is the case, then I suggest you examine the root causes and see which speech patterns you are engaged in that may be leading others to interrupt you!

Conversations that include interruptions, whatever the root cause, become choppy and convoluted, and no participants get to fully express themselves. Instead, the conversation is competitive, like sparring. Pick your combat sport. A conversation full of interruption is like a boxing or wrestling match full of punches and counter punches. Interrupting facilitates arguments and disagreements because no one gets the chance to complete a thought, and moreover, negative emotions come into play like anger, anxiety, and even depression. Do you reach better solutions or consensus with incomplete thoughts and interruptions? Tell me the last time you changed someone's mind in an argument or "competitive conversation." You can't think of a situation because competitive conversation doesn't work to progress thinking and decision-making. All it does is feed the egos of the combatants.

Interrupting is the ultimate arrogant and selfish act. Learning not to interrupt someone is part of pre-school or kindergarten education. It is a lesson right up there with taking turns and learning to share. These are some of the earliest lessons we probably remember. We know better. And as with any change in behavior, there is a positive halo effect on other behaviors you have. Interrupt less and you are likely to be generally less rude and less aggressive, and likely learn more from those around you. So pay attention to these root causes and watch out for them before they happen. And if you find yourself interrupted often, check yourself for the root causes. If you can think of interrupting as the equivalent of banging the bottom of an old ketchup bottle, then you understand how the victims of interrupting feel. Great listening, like great ketchup, is worth the wait. There. Now I am done and I would love to hear your opinion. Thanks for not interrupting.

How to Listen to Your Angry Boss

Some people don't like the word "boss." We like to use terms like "leader," "team lead," and "manager." But everybody has a boss. Even if you are a CEO, you have a board, shareholders, customers and government agencies. Most of us have a traditional boss. While it can sometimes be difficult to know who your boss is in a world where we try to avoid the term in favor of egalitarian terminology (we are all "contributors," "associates," "team mates" and "coworkers"), at the end of the day, you have a boss. Your boss is the person who gives you raises and bonuses (or not); the person who can get you fired, promoted, or recommend that you be; and the person who manages your work effort—what you do and when. When you think about it, your boss has a lot of power. That is one reason they and the term are so disliked. I have had many bosses during the past 30 years and, like most of us, I have also been a boss. If there is one person you want to listen well to and understand, it is your boss.

Bosses can be hard to listen to and understand. They may say left and we are thinking right. A boss may say, "Please do it this way," and we think, "What are they thinking?" A boss may say do it this way today, and then another way the next day. On occasion, we are certain we did exactly what they asked and then they criticize our work. And when they are angry? How hard is it to listen to an angry boss? For many of us, we have or have had bosses who (at least at times) are downright opaque, obscure and abstract.

I never appreciated abstract art, but I am getting better at it. And the same path that helped me better understand abstract art has helped me with bosses, and with being a better boss. I bought a modern painting recently, a Daniel Maltzman, which I like, and I see something different every time I look at it. And doesn't that sound like some of our bosses—or all bosses—at least some of the time? A different "element" or facet of their personality presents itself as they attempt to fulfill their own organizational role.

My appreciation of modern art required me to separate the art into two roles. The first role was functional: to fit somewhere structurally that worked in a room. For example, the size has to accentuate the space in the room. The colors should accentuate or complement or contrast with the colors already in the room or with outside colors. Modern art plays a functional role in a house, apartment, condominium or museum. The second and very distinctive aspect of the art is the personality of the piece. In essence, you need to listen to the painting and feel its movement and elements to appreciate it. I like to imagine what the artist did first and second, and even the look on their face as they painted it. I like to know who they are, where they are from, what they might be thinking. I like to understand the context of their work. And if you do some research and study the artist, you will find the commonalities—the elements that make works identifiable as theirs.

If a boss were a machine—all function and no personality or human element—what would that be like? Those who watched "Star Trek" know. Leonard Nimoy, aka Spock, who lived long and prospered until recently, played the boss, with only function and no human element. And while I am not a complete "Trekkie," I watched the show all the time in my youth. Captain Kirk (think CEO), played by William Shatner, was full of emotion and personality. Until we work for robots, Shatner is the representative model for bosses, not Spock. Sure, Captain Kirk had a job and function, but he also had a strong personality and was full of emotion.

If you want to be better at listening to and understanding your boss, like appreciating an abstract painting, you have to separate the two parts—function and personality—as you listen. You have to filter and divide functional needs and instruction from the personality element. Your boss has a functional role in the organization and your boss is a human being with personality, movement and characteristics that make him or her a unique human being. Learning to listen well to your boss requires you to separate each of these two elements: functional role and human expression. Your boss has a role in the organization and your boss has a boss. The pressures you feel and the communication you get from your boss reflect what they are functionally accountable for, and to whom. Your work, in a well-structured organization, is part of the work that your boss is accountable for to his or her boss, and the organizational goals. A good boss and a good organization will help you understand how your work helps with the organization's mission and objectives. If your boss was just a cog in the organizational machine and had no personality or emotion, you would be working for Spock. But you don't.

Here are some tips for listening to your boss and separating the functional from the emotional.

- ***Learn how your boss expresses what is really important to them.*** Everyone has different communication styles. But even when angry, especially when angry, they operate out of habit. What is their habit of conveying what is really important? This can best be discovered when you are given more than one thing to do. Always ask which is the most important and see how they convey that to you. Some bosses, especially in New York and the Northeast, will say it twice or even three times. Others (I have seen this among more introverted bosses and in the Midwest) will mutter it under their breath. You won't know what is important if you don't know what is really important to your boss. So consciously asking them to prioritize your multiple assignments and listening and watching their response will teach you how they speak differently about what is important and what is not. I had a boss from the Midwest who would talk and talk and talk, and then at the end mutter something under their breath. I learned over time that the final mutter is what they really thought, and the most important thing to them.

- ***Don't ignore the emotional personality, but don't take it personally either.*** Objectives and timelines create immediate pressure. Your boss has objectives and timelines and hands some off to you and the rest to others in her or his organization. Something doesn't get done on time? Something doesn't get done right? Boom. Emotion is a way to release stress. Understanding the emotional personality of your boss is critical, so don't ignore it but don't absorb it. As Mr. Miyagi always said, "When punch comes don't be there." Just listen, and as you listen, separate any helpful advice or criticism from personal attack. I once had a boss who was so mad she literally threw a file at me. When I picked it up and said, "I can't believe you threw a file at me," she said, "I didn't. As I recall I set it in your lap and you stood up." It can be hard to separate yourself from someone else's tantrum, but you have to do it. Obviously, extreme cases may need to be reported to HR as well as any matter that involves discrimination of a protected class. As a 30-something white male at the time, I chalked it up to something I might write about someday. And now I have.

- ***To handle an emotional outburst from your boss requires breaking some of the usual listening rules.*** Never, ever try to practice active listening if your boss is yelling or in another emotional state. Never say, "So, boss, what you are trying to say is I screwed up." Don't repeat the criticism. Your best bet is to separate the emotion from the message and not take it personally. Nod at anything you agree with and don't nod if you disagree. During an emotional outburst, most of the communication is non-verbal. Your boss is using body language, tone, volume and other tactics to communicate displeasure. Believe it or not, they don't necessarily know what they are saying. But even in a tirade, there can be helpful nuggets, so be listening for them.
- ***Learn how to practice listening triage and convert the right sounds to background noise.*** At some point in your life you learned how to stratify sounds. You treat some sounds as background noise and some sounds your ears almost wiggle to hear. This is actually a survival skill. If you are in the woods, some sounds make your heart beat fast and cause your adrenal glands to ramp up. Other sounds are relaxing, comforting and safe. In our early ancestors' days, if you got those two wrong you could be dinner for a predator. You need to practice separating functional and emotional messages. I hung out with Lawrence Tynes, a now-retired NFL placekicker, one night after a fundraiser golf tournament in Scotland. He

recounted a missed field goal against Green Bay in the NFL playoffs, which I had seen on TV. I remember the Giants coach just screaming at him as he returned to the sidelines. Together, he and I watched the clip from his interview with David Letterman. Letterman asked him what the coach was saying when he was screaming and yelling at Tynes. Tynes said, "I never hear what he is saying. I know he is yelling at me, I just never hear him." He goes on to explain he never lets one missed kick get him down. I asked him how he handled the pressure. He said, "It's just a game, Cash." If you have a volatile boss, watch David Letterman's video interview of Lawrence Tynes on not letting it get to you.

- ***Don't argue with constructive criticism.*** When someone goes on offense, we tend to go on defense. Playing offense/ defense with your boss is not in your best interest. Don't shut down either. Take it in and consider it, even if it makes you angry and you completely disagree. Use body language for feedback rather than getting into an argument. Give yourself time to consider the criticism or advice. There might be something to it. Discuss it with your friend or significant other; they may actually agree with your boss. And if you receive valid criticism, turn it into a "to-do" item. Take a sticky note and put it on your monitor or somewhere you will be reminded of it so you can work on it.

- ***If you handle your boss's outburst well, they owe you one.*** I remember when I was a young lawyer, a very powerful person screamed at me because I was questioning a transaction. How powerful? He was the CEO of my company and former Cabinet Member in the White House who had come out of the Reagan administration. I listened. It was hard not to argue or defend myself. He was actually wrong and should have listened to me. Instead, he blasted me. I just listened. Months later I bumped into the CEO, and he was with Henry Kissinger, having dinner. He introduced me to Kissinger. He was polite as if nothing had happened. Word got back to me that he felt bad about "yelling at that young lawyer." I forgave the heat of the moment and it was good for me later. It resulted in admiration from my peers, who'd heard about it, and I was promoted to a new opportunity.

As long as humans work for humans, there will be functional roles and personalities in our interactions. Bosses are human—sometimes too human. But understanding your boss and listening to your boss requires patience, separating the emotional content from the helpful content, not taking it personally and not arguing about it. Use body language to provide feedback in emotional scenarios. You won't win an argument and even if you do, you may do permanent damage to the relationship. Bosses can be like abstract art, where you find yourself discovering new facets all too frequently. And based on my experience, some of the most difficult bosses are found in some of the most fascinating functions, and you can learn a lot more from them than the "hands-off" types. But to manage your boss, you have to know how to listen to your boss and learn their communication style over time. While nothing justifies a boss's disrespectful behavior to a subordinate or employee, it happens. So you need to be prepared for it when it does, and know how to extract any benefit while minimizing damage to your self-esteem.

Frosty, The Taz, and Listening to Introverts

Frosty the Snowman and the Tasmanian Devil were two fictitious characters that pervaded my childhood like some other characters did. I liked and probably mirrored the Tasmanian Devil's appetite, energy level and personality. Frosty the Snowman was just a snowman that came to life and then ran around the town with the kids. Frosty, at least in my childhood, was motionless and lifeless until they put a silk hat on him and he came to life. The "Taz" was an outgoing, grunting, growling, active animal, rumored to have been based in part on Errol Flynn. For purposes of listening, I am going to call Frosty an introvert and Taz an extrovert. If you want to learn how to listen better, you have to know whether you are dealing with Frosty or Taz in your conversation, because they require completely different sets of listening skills.

When did you first hear the terms introvert and extrovert? When and where were you first labeled an introvert or an extrovert? Take your time and try to recall it. It is one of those early labels that gets applied to each and every one of us. I was a Taz, so I got the label of extrovert very early. I want to say it was in Pittsburgh and I was in 2nd grade at Atlantic Avenue Elementary School. The school has since been torn down, but my memories of it and especially Mrs. Clausen are fresh. Mrs. Clauson, my second-grade teacher, washed my mouth out with soap once because at the age of 6, I heard a rhyme from a fellow pupil and I wouldn't tell her what he said. She finally demanded I tell the whole class. It was a silly rhyme: "Tra La La Boomsiay, I took your pants away; while you were standing there, I took your underwear." I don't really know what it means to this day; it was just a stupid rhyme passed among classmates, but the minute I said "underwear," she hauled me off to the lavatory and made me put soap in my mouth. One easy extrovert test: If you have ever had your mouth washed out with soap, you are an extrovert. On my next report card I got a 3 on a scale of 1-3 on self-discipline--the worst you could get--and she wrote, "Talks too much" in the comments. My parents had to sign that. Straight As and a 3. I became a lawyer. Go figure.

In my youth, pretty much all of my friends were extroverts and we avoided introverts. There were plenty of both. We just didn't understand why those introverts had nothing to say. They just sat there, staring at the blackboard or at us. And to be honest, I think we kind of shunned them and maybe even made fun of them. Some of them were so shy they didn't even respond when teachers called on them. They had nothing to say, so why bother? Introverts seemed to hang out with each other or just be alone together, and that was just fine with us extroverts. So, we didn't talk to each other and didn't listen to each other. How could we when they refused to talk?

It wasn't as if I reflected on this back then as I am now, but I was forced to when I was 28 years old. Fast-forward 22 years or so from 2nd grade to age 28, and I was about to become the General Manager of Union Pacific ExpressAir, a subsidiary of Union Pacific Railroad, which was headquartered in St. Louis. At 28 I was going to be the youngest employee of that division and in charge. And so the Railroad figured they would send me to leadership school. I was sent to The Center for Creative Leadership, which had a week-long session scheduled for me at Eckerd College in St. Petersburg, Florida. I had to take a battery of tests before I went, then I spent a week in a variety of sessions to learn to "lead." At the end of the week, you were analyzed on a comprehensive basis, including peer reviews from attendees from the other companies and a boatload of psychologists and organizational behavior scientists. What do you think my biggest leadership shortfall was? Surprise! All the experts agreed that I discriminated against introverts.

One of the introverted members of my peer group wrote a long essay about me and then confronted me in person in front of the psychologists, saying he could tell I didn't like him and that I never listened to him. I countered, getting animated, almost "Taz like," and I said, "Mike (of course, I don't remember his actual name), we were in survival exercises on the moon, we were trying to solve a puzzle, we were trying to decide who to put on a rocketship to send to Mars to start a new world —-all these challenges-—and you said NOTHING!" Mike looked at me, bewildered, as if I were an idiot and said, "You never asked." Well, that was it. I thought he was crazy and he thought I was nuts. We sat and stared at each other for a while and I finally said I was sorry. I had no idea. I don't remember his apologizing, but I would have had to ask for that, I guess.

But that lesson, that lesson in listening and in leadership, has stayed with me. And here is one of the most important listening skills you need to develop. You need to know whether you are sitting across from the Taz or Frosty. If you aren't communicating well with Taz, you aren't listening. If you aren't communicating well with Frosty, you aren't asking. Listening to introverts doesn't mean waiting for them to say something. They might not. You need to engage them by asking questions and then more questions.

And here is the risk for the leader who fails to ask an introvert. There are studies that show introverts are more intelligent. I will settle for this: They are just as intelligent and may see things in different ways. It is a form of diversity in team building to have both introverts and extroverts on a project or team, or in a meeting. But you have to ask them to "listen" to them. You want to know another introvert trait? They tend to be great listeners. They aren't focusing on what to say next—they are listening.

RE-CAP: BROWN BELT LISTENING TECHNIQUES

- ***Shut up and sell.*** Learn the power of silence and practice it. Bite your tongue. Let words sit and float in the air. Let people digest what someone has said. Breathe your way through the temptation to talk.
- ***Ask and listen.*** Learn to pivot from no. When you hear the word "no," don't argue, ask. Ask and listen, and then ask some more and listen some more.
- ***Mind drift.*** Develop techniques for avoiding mind drift. Mind drift often results from external distractions. Avoid them. Practice focus and concentration.
- ***Say this, not that.*** Be conscious of the implied manipulation of your responses. Carefully select your responses when you are listening.
- ***Ego.*** Practice not thinking about your position as someone speaks. Try to make it not about you.
- ***Understand the root causes of interrupting.*** Interrupting others is a selfish and arrogant action. Be aware of the causes and avoid them. Don't be a dominator. If you are a dominator, eventually you will find yourself with only one listener: You.

BLACK BELT

PUTTING TECHNIQUES TOGETHER AND MASTERING BASICS

Black belts don't practice single techniques; they practice routines full of techniques. They also revisit all of the basics and reach a deeper understanding of what they learned earlier. Beginning with the essay "Love Song Lyrics and Listening Skills," we revisit listening challenges in the context of remembering our favorite songs. We are good on rhythm, but lousy on lyrics. We now train ourselves to have a pre-listening routine, a set of the techniques we have learned, that we perform before we are to listen to someone. Next, we delve into topics designed to help get us in the moment, the true calling of a black belt. The black belt trains on internal dialogue in "Listening to Your Self-Talk." The final listening essay, "Breathing and Listening," is about breathing. Although breathing is our initial act in life, it is taken for granted, and like listening, it's another life skill that is not taught. Yet, if you learn to breathe properly, everything becomes clearer and easier.

Love Song Lyrics and Listening Skills

I have heard some great bar bets in my day and they are fun. A bar bet is any bet that is more challenging and more fun when you have a drink in your hand. Living in Texas for many years now, my current favorite is, "Which is closer to El Paso, Texas—Dallas, Texas or the California border?" Of course, it is the latter. Lately, as I am studying and writing about listening this year, in lieu of a bar bet, I have been asking people to recite the lyrics of their favorite song.

As Valentine's Day is upon us, I like to ask people what their favorite love song is. It doesn't have to be a new song. I prefer it isn't. I prefer it's one they have heard many times—maybe 100. Do you know what is a safe bar bet? They can't recite very much of the lyrics even though they have heard the song 100 times. I have the same problem. Why can't we remember the lyrics? And this isn't age-related. Young people are no better. We all get the melody and maybe a few lines from the chorus and then we hum. So it isn't a memory issue—it is a listening issue. What can we learn about listening from our inability to recite the lyrics to love songs we have heard hundreds of times?

In my opinion, it is because we aren't really paying attention. We tune in and out. When the song comes on, we are doing something else. It is background for us. Maybe we are trying to put an arm around a loved one. Maybe the song is part of a movie we are watching. And so when I ask you the words, you remember a few and then you hum. Most of us hum the song pretty well. The reason we can do that is that the music is on the right side of our brain, which actually has a higher IQ than the left side where language is processed. Try it now. How many of the lyrics of your favorite loves songs can you recite? And there is a lesson here. We aren't focusing on the lyrics, or focusing enough. And repetition doesn't help because we are no more focused the 100th time. And yet, if I sat you down with the song and said, "Listen to the lyrics and I am going to test you afterwards," you would be amazed at how many you would be able to recall after just a few repetitions. Try it. Now ask yourself: In your daily conversations, how much of them do you treat like background noise? I know the answer I would get if I asked your significant other.

If you want to be a great listener, you need to focus on it and actually prepare yourself to listen. Let's call it "pre-listening." Think about how you prepare for something you consider really important. It is Valentine's Day tomorrow. Your significant other or wife or husband is going to judge you on how you do. And it won't be how many roses or how much the jewelry is or how nice or expensive the restaurant is. Right? It will be how much time, effort and planning you put into whatever you do. Nothing says "I love you" like running by Whole Foods to pick up flowers on your way home. Anyone can do that. And many of us do. Maybe Valentine's Day is a silly holiday. But regardless of how you feel about

Hallmark, our society has us conditioned to consider what our loved one does for us on that day. If you don't think it matters, don't do anything and see how that works for you. Preparation is what we evaluate. We want effort. We say, "It's the thought that counts," and that confirms my point. The "thought" refers to the caring and preparation and effort. So what effort and preparation are you putting into your listening experiences?

Pre-listening is like any other preparation. It means you take the speaker or other person in the conversation seriously, and really want to take in the content and deal with it. So here are some pre-listening tips that will help you succeed in sales, your career, your relationships and any other activity involving another human being:

- ***Spend time studying the person with whom you will engage.*** If you don't know them, look them up. Get some background information from people who have engaged with them. If you know them, understand where they are right now. What are they dealing with in their company? We always say, "Know your audience," when we think about a talk or speech we are going to give. Well, if you are listening, part of pre-listening is to know your speaker! I am done when someone gets an appointment with me and says, "Tell me about your company." Really, all the tools you have available to you, and you say that! That tells me you have done nothing. You are "winging it."

- ***Remove distracting items from your person and surroundings.*** I have been selling since I was 12—11, actually—when I had a newspaper route in Pittsburgh, Pennsylvania. I sold newspapers door to door. I always used the holiday papers to get people to subscribe. I showed up at the door with a holiday or Sunday edition of the *Pittsburgh Post-Gazette* in my hands and nothing else. I can't imagine showing up with a cell phone and talking on the phone while I waited for someone to come to the door. Don't even consider bringing a PDA to a sales call. I have some defense clients where you can't bring a cell phone with a camera into the facility. I love that rule. Check your PDA at the door.
- ***Clear your mind of your own issues.*** We are always thinking about many things. Just ask yourself what you are thinking about and your mind will tell you. It is all those uncertainties, fears and lists of things to do in our heads. Distraction is the major impediment to listening, remembering and success. And if you are on a sales call or at some other important meeting, distraction is obvious. Your face shows it and your body language shows it. How to clear your mind? Before that important meeting or call, get yourself a piece of paper or your favorite app and write a list of everything you think is on your mind. Now tell yourself you will return to it after the meeting or sales call.

- ***Multi-tasking and listening do not go well together.*** You aren't focused on the lyrics of your love song, you are focused on other things and even seduced by some of them, like the melody. One of the absolute smartest people I have ever met was a lawyer at Jenner & Block. He wasn't the most successful for other reasons, but he was the smartest. You could walk into his office doorway and start to talk. He would not look up and he would not acknowledge you. He would finish what he was reading or writing, no matter how long it took, and then he would ask you what you wanted. This guy could remember file numbers that were 14 digits long. And he remembered everything everyone ever said. I bet he knew the lyrics to many love songs.
- ***An open-door policy has drawbacks.*** I hadn't remembered my fellow lawyer mentioned above until I wrote this, but starting next week I am going to do better at the whole "open-door" thing. We executives like to take pride in an open door. Why? It shows we are approachable and open. That's great, but if we don't listen well, it is just a concept and even insincere. So an open-door policy needs to be accompanied by, "I am open to you but wait until I finish what I am dong." You are really cheating two people when you multi-task: the one you are writing an email to and the one at your door.
- ***Have a "pre-listening" routine.*** Great competitors have routines they follow. Watch golfers before they swing for

real. They have a certain number and style of pre-swings. Some will open and close a glove to hear the velcro to get themselves set. These are champions trying to do the same thing the same way every time. Your pre-listening routine may include turning off your cell phone, making your list of what is distracting you inside your head, and spending time studying and preparing for the people you will be encountering in the meeting or call. Follow this every time to be a champion listener and closer.

On Valentine's Day, or any day, what a great day to kick off a new pre-listening routine. Clear your mind with a list of everything that could distract you until you can't write anymore because you are out of items. Put your cell phone aside (after you call your mother) and eliminate items that compete for your attention. Put your PDA to bed while you stay up. Learn to clear your mind by making a list of everything that is on your mind and scheduling a time to come back to it. Important to-dos are real and our survival nature will cause them to keep popping up in our head until we're sure we will deal with them later. In the office on Monday, keep your door open, but don't degrade two conversations to show how open you are. And finally, while you are at it, take some time to absorb the lyrics of your favorite love song.

Listening to Your Self-Talk

Everyone has a form of self-talk. This is the internal dialogue that goes on in our heads that we don't share with others. Or do we? How you are talking to yourself at any given moment is reflected on your face and in your body language. You can easily test this. Sit across from a close friend or significant other and think about something horrible. Within minutes your partner or friend will say, "What's wrong?" You simply cannot hide your internal self. It is so difficult to hide your inside on the outside that there are great skills, matches—contests, if you will—to see who can do it best. They are called poker games. You don't realize it because you have the handicap of not being able to see it. But everyone else does see it and does feel it. And researchers have shown that the difference between constructive and destructive self-talk matters (Rogelberg, UNC study).

Given that you are engaged in self-talk there are two separate consequences. First, your self-talk affects how talkers perceive you as they speak to you. And second, your self-talk can be a major source of distraction, impeding your listening. Step one is to become aware of your self-talk.

Some people consciously talk to themselves. Most of us are aware of it from time to time. If you are less conscious of it, the best way to raise awareness of your self-talk is probably to focus on the most extreme forms of it. For me, that is when I do something wrong in a golf swing or other activity. I find myself saying, "Why did you do that?" It can also be when you hurt someone's feelings or say something stupid or something you wish you hadn't. "What was I thinking?" Or it may be after something goes well. You kill it in a meeting. You hit the ball well. Now you say, "You Da Man." The point is to catch yourself when you do self-talk and gradually become aware of your inner dialogue.

The best way to understand the impact of your self-talk is to look at pictures of yourself. Now that everyone carries a camera in the form of a phone, everyone has his or her picture taken more often. Look at pictures of yourself and remember the occasions. If you are happy on the inside, you are happy on the outside. Look at your facial expression. What would you say to you? What were you saying to yourself?

Study your face relaxed. Especially if you are older, your face reflects habits and muscle movements you have performed over the years. If you want to be a good listener, you need to know what your face is saying to those speaking to it. You can change your naturally appearing face by conscious effort and by taking control of your inner dialogue. You also need to change your actions to help change your inner dialogue. If you are looking naturally sad, go to more weddings and christenings and fewer funerals. Spend more time with happy people and less time with sad people.

Dale Carnegie's age-old tips on how to win friends and influence people are great for listening tips. Do you know what one of his top-10 tips was? Smile. I am always amazed at people who think others don't like them. They never seem happy, don't smile, wear a constant negative look and then think other people don't like them. When it comes to facial exchanges, you get what you give. When people smile at you, frown at them. Watch how quickly their smile disappears. We are a collection of walking mirrors that can't see ourselves, but see others clearly.

You will be challenged to be a good listener if you have negative self-talk. People will hold back on you because you appear judgmental. You simply will not get the best out of others if you intimidate them. To listen well, you need to not bring judgment to the party. You need to smile, give yourself some positive self-talk and listen.

Finally, you can't listen well if your mind is full of self-talk. You need to empty your mind. If you are talking to yourself, you are multi-tasking with the person speaking with you. Multi-tasking is the death of paying attention—by definition.

Breathing and Listening

The first thing we do when we are born is breathe. If we don't, we get a slap so we are forced to breathe. The last thing we do before we die is take our last breath. And who helps us learn to breathe between our first and last breath? Nobody. It is considered something that is an auto response. It is considered programmatic. Unless you are a professional athlete, the only encounters you may have with breathing lessons are yoga, meditation and martial arts. As a result, most don't realize the power of breathing patterns and the power that can come from working with your breathing.

In Karate we learned to discharge a powerful breath as we completed a move. This is the part of the purpose of the Kiai that you hear karate practitioners make when they are completing a strike. The problem with this breathing technique is it often causes you to hold your breath. When your breath stops, your movement stops, your mind stops and everything comes to a halt.

My truly advanced training in breathing didn't come until I studied Systema, the Russian Martial Art. I recommend the book Secrets of the Russian Breath Masters, by Vladimir Vasiliev. I have trained for nearly a decade under Vladimir and a lot of this martial art surrounds breathing. Proper breathing brings proper movement, relaxation and readiness.

Controlling your breathing helps control your self-talk, which affects the vibe, aura, call it what you will, that you give off to a speaker in a conversation, and your ability to absorb information through speech or other senses. While not a substitute for reading Vladimir's book, here are a few key principles I have learned studying Systema and reading Vladimir's book.

- ***Become conscious of your breathing.*** Be aware of your breathing. Check yourself. Here is what I found about my breathing: When I am tense, I take short breaths. When I am relaxed, long breaths. So if you want to be relaxed, slow your breathing. If you want to energize yourself, short breaths.
- ***Breathe in through your nose and out through your mouth.***
- ***Feel your body react to your breathing and what muscles are engaged.***
- ***As you do exercises or any daily activities, be conscious of your in-and-out breathing.*** If you swing a golf club try breathing in on the back swing and breathing out on the swing.
- ***Be conscious of holding your breath.*** When we are startled, we hold our breath. The first time I met Vladimir and I sat down in a chair he said, "You held your breath." And he was right, I did. Just the act of sitting down in a chair interrupted my life and movement and thinking. Don't hold your breath!

- ***Breathe continuously.*** Don't stop breathing.
- ***Make your breathing natural;*** don't take in any more air than you need.
- ***We do walking exercises that can help beginners.*** As you take a step, breathe in and then take another step and breathe out. You can extend these to two steps breathing in, and two steps breathing out, and mix them up.

You really need the help of a practitioner here to get advanced, but you will be a better listener if you can get control of your breathing and breath patterns. And as you become conscious of your own patterns, guess what happens? You will become conscious of the breath patterns of others, thereby allowing you to understand where they are coming from in a much deeper way. Become aware of yourself and you will "disappear." Once you disappear, the people around you will seem larger than life and their actions and words will appear louder than you can imagine. You will hear everyone.

The Systema people offer a camp every year in the woods north of Toronto. We focus on breathing and studying others. When I return to the corporate world from that week-long camp, the world sounds noisy to me for months afterwards. You need to find yourself a place to get away and clear your mind if you want to be a better listener. Vacations are great places to practice listening techniques.

RE-CAP: BLACK BELT LISTENING TECHNIQUES

- ***Develop a pre-listening routine.*** Have an established set of principles you follow before listening to someone. The PDA goes off, you research the talker, you write a list of what is in your head in order to clear your mind, you focus on your breathing, you check yourself for tension. You put all the techniques together to empty yourself so you can feel and truly listen to the other person.
- ***Master the art of listening to introverts.*** Practice conversing with quiet and shy folks. Work to engage them and learn what makes them excited to speak. They don't speak much so when they do, it will tell you a lot.
- ***Document the conversational style of those you listen to frequently.*** Understanding that people have different communication styles and recording what you learn from each engagement is invaluable to making you a black belt listener. Keep a journal of your insights and study it before you engage with them the next time.
- ***Eliminate the practice of multi-tasking.*** This does a disservice to both the person whose email you are reading and the person at your door. Explain to whoever is at your "open door" that you need a minute to finish what you are doing.
- ***Control your self-talk.*** Pay attention to what you say to yourself and make it more positive over time.

- ***Control your breathing.*** Become aware and train your breathing so you can improve your ability to take in information.
- ***Disappear.*** Get to know yourself so deeply that you can erase yourself and only feel and hear the other person.

CONCLUSION

Listening, like breathing, are skills we take for granted and do not teach. There is academic research about a variety of topics, but very little in the way of guides to being a better listener. Listening is a key survival skill in our modern world and we listen poorly, but think we are good at it. This is the worst of all worlds. We are in denial about our listening.

When we are young, we are taught that we are bad listeners through childhood games. But then our teachers do nothing about it. It is an accepted life-skill deficiency. Do you remember the game "telephone?" I do. In elementary school and at several other times in my life in educational settings we played "telephone." It goes by other names. All the children get in a line or a circle. The teacher tells a phrase to the first person, like telling a secret. The first one passes the secret to the next and then the next. At the end, the final child tells the teacher the phrase. Surprise! It bears little relationship to the secret that started. But what do we do about it? Nothing. We are simply left with the lesson that we should be skeptical about hearsay.

We live in a world of talkers, writers and speakers. But based on my experience in the social, legal and business world, the successful folks are great listeners. If you bought this book, you have decided to improve your listening skills. Congratulations.

I am not a professional researcher and do not have the bandwidth to be both a constant practitioner and observer and a researcher. But test these methods and decide for yourself their merit. Your listening improvement journey is your personal journey. My hope is that I have intrigued you enough to be a better leader, salesperson, manager, negotiator and all-around person by honing your listening skills. If you find something works or doesn't, please write me at cash@cashnickerson.com. I look forward to hearing from you.

Choosing Who You Listen to

Not all speakers are created equally. One choice you make is who to interact with and when. I like to listen to great people because they influence how I view the world and ultimately my self-talk and listening skills. Great speakers are easier to listen to as they are great listeners; they know how to speak so you will hear. I am a shameless patriot and enjoy reading documents that are the foundation of our democracy. What follows is an essay about something I noticed about our Declaration of Independence as I read it July 4, 2015.

Listening to Greatness: The Fearless Fifty-Six Signers

Each year, on the Fourth of July, I read our Constitution and the Declaration of Independence. Last year I read my passport for the first time and wrote about it. "When We Leave the Home of the Brave" is an essay about the inherent freedom to travel. (It appears as a chapter in my book *Getting to Next.*) Maybe it is the lawyer in me or maybe it is just my profound respect for our freedoms. In any event, each year as I read the documents, I find something I haven't seen before, even after all these years.

This year's July 4th celebrations are overshadowed by vague and ominous terrorist threats, which we hope and pray do not come to fruition. But our country was founded by those who faced tyranny and terrorism. They found their strength in bonding together and pledging allegiance to each other and their country, and also relied on "Divine Providence" to support what they knew was right. Here is the last sentence of the Declaration in case you haven't read it lately.

"And for the support of this declaration, with a firm reliance on the protection of Divine Providence, we mutually pledge to each other our lives, our fortunes and our sacred honor."

What I discovered this year that I had not previously seen was that one of the signers, and only one, put where he was from after his name: Charles Carroll of Carrollton. I must confess I didn't remember him from any of the history I learned in Pittsburgh or Minneapolis or even upstate New York. And you might not either unless you live in Maryland or are Catholic, because he was a big deal in Maryland and one of the first Catholic politicians at a time when Catholics were forbidden from holding political office, at least in Maryland. But I have now learned much about him from my research online. This man was probably the richest man in America and had maybe the most to lose in signing on to the Declaration. But not only did he sign; he told King George exactly where he could be found. And if you don't remember the harsh words of the Declaration, here are some that would have put every signer on King George's hit list.

"A prince, whose character is thus marked by every act which may define a tyrant, is unfit to be the ruler of a free people."

I just imagine the King reading that line and saying, "That's it. The Colonies are out of control. Find and arrest these signers for high treason. Off with their heads." Our founders found strength by bonding together and pledging allegiance to each other and their country. In thinking about how fundamental this was to our country's founding, I am reminded of the great Benjamin Franklin quote, "We must, indeed, all hang together or, most assuredly, we will all hang separately." That sounds like a path to greatness emanating from a profound dedication to team work, and it has been. Resolute and good people standing up to terrorist threats and tyranny are the very foundation of our United States. Whatever comes this July 4th, and hopefully nothing untoward, we will bond together and resolutely destroy the senseless evils that oppose us and our way of life.

Freedoms seem especially in focus this year as we have witnessed the Supreme Court on the one hand, and horrible, tragic events on the other, combine to reshape how we think about freedom and fundamental human rights. And these events are reminders that there are inequalities that remain in our country that we still need to address. We will face terrorism. And too many in the world face tyranny. So our thoughts and prayers must be with those countless thousands who have no freedom because they are refugees or captives or otherwise wrongfully confined, and with those in our own country who still seek a level playing field. Today, remember the fearlessness with which 56 people signed our Declaration of Independence. Remember and read about Charles Carroll of Carrollton, who, after thumbing his nose at King George, gave the King his address.

Happy July 4th and God Bless the United States of America.

ABOUT THE AUTHOR

Steven "Cash" Nickerson is President and a Principal of PDS Tech, Inc., a position he has held for 12 years. With approximately $400 million in annual sales, PDS is one of the largest engineering and IT staffing firms in the United States, employing more than 10,000 staffers annually. He has held a variety of legal and executive positions in his 30 year career, including serving as an attorney and marketing executive for Union Pacific Railroad, an associate and then partner at Jenner & Block, one of Chicago's five largest law firms and chairman and CEO of an internet company he took public through a reverse merger.

An avid writer and speaker on the workplace, the jobs economy and employment, Mr. Nickerson is the author of *BOOMERangs, Engaging the Aging Workforce in America* (2014), *StagNation, Understanding the New Normal in Employment* (2013) and *Getting To Next, Lessons to Help Take Your Career to The Next Level* (2015). He also writes travel books, including, *A Texan in Tuscany* (2013).

Mr. Nickerson holds a JD and MBA from Washington University in St. Louis, where he was an editor of the law review and a recipient of the US Steel Scholarship. He is a member of the National Council of the Washington University in St. Louis School of Law and International Council of the Whitney R. Harris World Law Institute. Mr. Nickerson serves on the Equifax Workforce Solutions Client Advisory Board and was Keynote speaker at the Equifax 2013 Client Forum. Mr. Nickerson was honored with the Distinguished Alumni Award in 2013 by Washington University in St. Louis School of Law and a Founders Day Distinguished Alumni Award from Washington University in St. Louis in 2014. He received the Global Philanthropy Award in 2010 from Washington University in St. Louis for his support of the Crimes Against Humanity Initiative. Mr. Nickerson was elected the Ethan A. H. Shepley Trustee at Washington University in St. Louis on December 5, 2014 for a four year term.

Mr. Nickerson is licensed to practice law in California, Nevada, Illinois, Nebraska and Texas and is a member of the American, Los Angeles, Austin and Dallas Bar Associations. He is an avid martial artist, ranked as a third degree black belt in Kenpo Karate, a Purple Belt in Brazilian Jiu Jitsu. He is also a Russian Martial Art instructor at his school, Big D Systema in Dallas.

Mr. Nickerson has appeared on numerous talk radio shows, including "NPR," "The Joe Elliot Show," "Americas Evening News," "Lifestyle Talk Radio," "The Lifestyle Show," "Conversations with Peter Solomon," "Ringside Politics," "The Dave Malarkey Show," "The Morning Show" and "The Costa Report."

ALSO BY CASH NICKERSON

Want to put your newfound listening skills to work? Read *Getting to Next: Lessons to Help Take Your Career to the Next Level,* available in print and affordable eBook formats. For insider info, advance notice about new titles, special discounts and giveaways, sign up for his mailing list at www.cashnickerson.com/mailing-list

Made in the USA
Coppell, TX
30 August 2022

82268396R00077